The Wilhelm Gustloff Story

by Michael Capek

Content Consultant

Milan Hauner

Honorary Fellow, History Department
University of Wisconsin–Madison

Famous *Ships*

Essential Library

An Imprint of Abdo Publishing | abdopublishing.com

abdopublishing.com

Published by Abdo Publishing, a division of ABDO, PO Box 398166, Minneapolis, Minnesota 55439. Copyright © 2018 by Abdo Consulting Group, Inc. International copyrights reserved in all countries. No part of this book may be reproduced in any form without written permission from the publisher. Essential Library™ is a trademark and logo of Abdo Publishing.

Printed in the United States of America, North Mankato, Minnesota
092017
012018

THIS BOOK CONTAINS
RECYCLED MATERIALS

Cover Photo: ullstein bild/Getty Images
Interior Photos: akg-images/Newscom, 4–5, 20, 24, 42–43, 48, 51, 67; RIA Novosti/Sputnik/AP Images, 6–7; akg-images/Rainer Hackenberg/Newscom, 10; TASS/Getty Images, 12; Alexei Mezhuyev/TASS/Getty Images, 15; Imagno/Hulton Archive/Getty Images, 18–19; HW Warhurst News Syndication/Newscom, 28; Berliner Verlag/Archiv/picture-alliance/dpa/AP Images, 30; ullstein bild/Getty Images, 32–33, 54–55, 78–79; Fred Ramage/Hulton Archive/Getty Images, 36; Ewald Hoinkis/ullstein bild/Getty Images, 39; London Express/Hulton Archive/Getty Images, 45; Red Line Editorial, 52, 92; United Archives/Pollmann/Bridgeman Art, 60; SZ Photo/Scherl/Bridgeman Art, 62–63, 64–65; Ricardo Reitmeyer/Shutterstock Images, 74–75; Jörg Schurig/picture-alliance/dpa/AP Images, 81; Sueddeutsche Zeitung Photo/Alamy, 84–85; Georg Wendt/dpa/picture-alliance/Newscom, 86–87; AP Images, 91; Thiel Christian/SIPA/Newscom, 94–95; TF2/HS1 WENN Photos/Newscom, 96

Editor: Arnold Ringstad
Series Designer: Craig Hinton

Publisher's Cataloging-in-Publication Data

Names: Capek, Michael, author.
Title: The Wilhelm Gustloff story / by Michael Capek.
Description: Minneapolis, Minnesota : Abdo Publishing, 2018. | Series: Famous ships | Includes online resources and index.
Identifiers: LCCN 2017946748 | ISBN 9781532113239 (lib.bdg.) | ISBN 9781532152115 (ebook)
Subjects: LCSH: World War (1939-1945)--Juvenile literature. | World War, 1939-1945--Evacuation of civilians--Juvenile literature. | World War, 1939-1945--Naval operations--Juvenile literature. | World War, 1939-1945--Baltic Sea--Juvenile literature.
Classification: DDC 940.531--dc23
LC record available at https://lccn.loc.gov/2017946748

Contents

One
Terror in East Prussia 4

Two
Strength through Joy 18

Three
Escaping the Front 32

Four
Boarding 42

Five
A Stormy Departure 54

Six
Death in the Baltic 62

Seven
The Struggle for Survival 74

Eight
A Forgotten Story 86

Timeline 98
Essential Facts 100
Glossary 102
Additional Resources 104
Source Notes 106
Index 110
About the Author 112

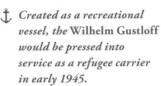

Chapter 1

TERROR IN EAST PRUSSIA

The *Wilhelm Gustloff* had not been to sea in several years. Its engines were stiff as the ship eased slowly away from the pier at Gotenhafen (now Gdynia, Poland). Aboard on that bitterly cold night of January 30, 1945, were approximately 10,000 people, crammed into every nook and cranny of a ship designed to carry only 1,500 passengers.[1]

The *Gustloff* had been designed and built for pleasure cruises to calm and sunny Mediterranean Sea isles and Norwegian fjords. It was never meant to sail in strong winds and choppy waves. The object of

⚓ *As the Red Army fought its way toward Germany in early 1945, it took revenge against not just the German military, but also civilians.*

this voyage on the stormy Baltic was not fun and relaxation, either. It was basic survival. That's why, although no one on board was particularly comfortable, every one of them felt incredibly fortunate. At least they were not among the terrified thousands of refugees still waiting and watching from the dark pier, praying another ship would come in time to carry them away before the Soviet Red Army arrived.

Horrific stories of Russian atrocities against German civilians had been circulating. For years, Russian and Polish citizens had endured unspeakable treatment from German soldiers. Now that German dictator Adolf Hitler's once powerful military was in retreat, it was payback time. When hate-maddened Russian soldiers stormed into East Prussia, the message was clear: No German man, woman, or child should expect any sort of kindness or mercy. Gruesome reports and pictures from

Seeking Revenge

"The long awaited hour, the hour of revenge is at hand! We all have personal reasons for revenge: my daughter, your sisters, our Mother Russia, the devastation of our land!"[2]

—*Soviet tank Colonel-General Pavel Rybalko to troops upon entering East Prussia in 1944*

towns and villages in East Prussia, now being liberated from German control by the Red Army, proved the warnings were more than empty threats.

The only chance for Germans, or anyone who had supported them, was to get out of the way. Hundreds of thousands of panic-stricken people had fled west ahead of the Russian onslaught, which was rapidly closing around them like the jaws of a massive vice. By the end of January 1945, vast numbers of refugees were trapped on the eastern shores of the Baltic Sea. If the remnants of the German navy could not muster enough ships to come and rescue them, the result might be the death of vast numbers of people.

That is why, as the *Wilhelm Gustloff* left the Bay of Danzig and turned west on the stormy, wind-whipped Baltic Sea, passengers began to feel things most of them had not felt in weeks. In spite of the cold and the seasickness and the cramped, smelly accommodations,

Operation Barbarossa

In June 1941, Germany invaded the Soviet Union in a massive military attack Hitler called Operation Barbarossa. German divisions seized huge tracts of land and unleashed unspeakable suffering on the Soviet people. Millions were deliberately starved to death or fell victim to other brutal German atrocities. More than 3 million Soviet prisoners of war died in German prison camps alone, and more than 1 million Soviet Jews were killed.[3] Ultimately, Barbarossa was a disaster for the German army, which suffered huge losses of soldiers, weapons, and machinery. It also drove the Soviets to the extreme acts of retaliation they exacted against East Prussia in 1945.

people began to feel relief and even a little hope. Perhaps their ordeal was nearly over.

Lone Wolf on the Prowl

The Soviet submarine captained by Commander Alexander Marinesko had the official designation *S-13*. In late 1944, the sub was stationed at a base in Turku, Finland. The powerful German air force kept Soviet subs penned there and at other bases, unable to operate. By the time the Allies finally regained air and sea superiority in 1944, Soviet sub commanders could not wait to get to sea and attack anything and everything flying the German flag.

In January 1945, Marinesko and his 46-man crew were relieved to finally be in action, cruising the Baltic Sea searching for German ships. For a while, *S-13* joined a group of subs that hunted and attacked together. But Marinesko had never liked taking orders from others.

Weapons of Undersea Warfare in World War II

Torpedoes were a submarine's most effective and deadly weapons. To combat them, many vessels had sonar, which allowed them to hear subs approaching underwater. That allowed ships to launch depth charges, bombs that exploded automatically at the depths where subs cruised. Ships and subs both had to deal with mines. These stationary bombs floated unseen beneath the surface until something came close or bumped them. An estimated 80,000 marine mines were scattered in the Baltic Sea during the war.[4] Specially equipped boats called minesweepers could safely explode or remove some mines, but not all. Many mines from the World War II era are still in the Baltic today, more than 70 years after the conflict ended.[5]

Alexander Marinesko

Commander

Commander Alexander Marinesko's resourcefulness and composure during deadly battle situations made him a legend in the Soviet submarine service. His accomplishments earned him the Combat Order of the Red Banner. During his career, however, Marinesko wasn't popular with Soviet officials, who didn't like his excessive drinking or insubordinate attitude. Such behavior in Soviet dictator Joseph Stalin's military was dangerous. Stalin was known for harsh crackdowns on his military officers. In January 1945, Marinesko understood that sinking enemy vessels was not just vital for his future as a sub commander. His life probably depended upon it. After the war, Marinesko was dishonorably discharged and spent nearly two years in prison for theft. Following his release, he worked tirelessly to clear his reputation. He died in 1963 and did not live to see his name restored. Decades later, he was posthumously awarded his nation's highest honor, Hero of the Soviet Union, in 1990.

He also didn't like the idea of sharing credit for sinking ships, either. He craved honor and glory for himself and his crew. His sub was loaded with 12 powerful torpedoes, self-propelled underwater missiles that sub crews could fire while submerged or while cruising on the surface. Marinesko was eager to use them.

In late January, Marinesko had received news of the German navy's massive evacuation of refugees and military personnel from East Prussia. Large numbers of ships would be coming and going in the Gulf of Danzig. That's where the best hunting would be, so that's where he took *S-13*.

S-13 searched the area for more than three weeks without spotting any targets. The sub often sat stationary on the sea bottom during the day to avoid detection. It surfaced at night to watch for passing ships. Marinesko was particularly skilled at maneuvering stealthily until he was in a position to fire his torpedoes. But first he had to find a worthy target.

Marinesko steered *S-13* to a position known as the Stolpe Bank, where a 24-mile-long (38.6 km) and ten-mile-wide (16 km) underwater shoal of gravel extended out into the Baltic.[6] The water there was relatively shallow, so ships avoided it, preferring to swing out into the deeper channel. It was not a safe place for a sub to launch an attack, either, but Marinesko

⚓ *The Soviet submarine S-56 belonged to the same class as Marinesko's S-13.*

suspected that lookouts on ships would not be watching for subs on the shallow shore side as they passed. That would give him the advantage he needed.

For several days, *S-13* waited and watched. Large ships had to emerge from the Bay of Danzig eventually, Marinesko reasoned. He was right.

At approximately seven o'clock on the evening of January 30, *S-13* surfaced just after dark. Lookouts took up positions on the sub's conning tower, sweeping the darkness for any glimmer of light, listening for any sound of approaching engines. It was a difficult and painful task. Waves crashed over the sub, soaking the lookouts. Windblown snow and ice pelted them like bullets. But their fear of their captain's wrath, should they miss a passing target, was far stronger than their discomfort from the subzero cold.

It wasn't long before one of the lookouts saw lights glimmering through a curtain of snow. The lights were clearly moving. A ship was approaching, perhaps more than one.

The captain immediately ordered the crew to battle stations and gave orders to submerge, but not all the way. He wanted to stay on the high conning tower to visually direct the attack. He also needed to reduce the chances of detection. The approaching vessels might have radar, and they would certainly have lookouts scanning the sea in all directions. Luckily for *S-13,* waves were high enough that night to hide a low-riding sub from radar. Lookouts would see waves cascading over the sub's hull and think it was the white foam of waves breaking over rocks.

S-13's hydrophone operator had been listening to the sounds of the approaching vessels and plotting their speeds and courses. He passed the information to the captain. One of them had two propellers. That meant it was a large ship.

A minute later, the curtain of snow lifted and a bright moon emerged from behind the clouds. Right in front of him, the captain saw an enormous ship. It was a sleek ocean liner with red and green navigation lights glittering prettily in the blackness. Marinesko had spotted the *Wilhelm Gustloff.* Another smaller vessel, a torpedo boat escort, was moving fast some distance ahead. No other battleship or cruiser was in sight. The big vessel was virtually defenseless.

For the next two hours, Marinesko maneuvered his partially submerged sub into a course directly parallel to the *Gustloff*'s. On the shallow shore side, only a short distance from land, it was an incredibly risky action. The sub could hit a mine. If it were spotted and had to submerge, it couldn't go down very far. It would be a sitting duck for depth charges or perhaps ramming by the escort ship.

Marinesko didn't care. He was desperate for a kill, and he was determined to risk anything to get his prize. He gave orders to accelerate and pushed a little ahead of the slow-moving liner. It wasn't even zigzagging, the way most ships did to make it harder for subs to get a good shot. The captain turned *S-13* until its bow was facing the *Gustloff*'s port side and let the sub coast

⚓ *Crews delicately loaded torpedoes into Soviet submarines before patrols.*

closer. He wanted to eliminate any possibility that his prey might escape. It was just past nine o'clock in the evening when the *Gustloff* drifted into the crosshairs of *S-13*'s aiming scope. Marinesko gave the order to fire four torpedoes in quick succession.

Aboard the *Gustloff*, most of the passengers were asleep. Several of the ship's officers had just sat down for something to eat. They'd been so busy and tense since their departure four hours earlier, plotting courses and bracing for trouble, that they had had no chance to relax. Now it appeared their voyage of hope was going to end well. They shared some sandwiches and hot cups of soup, toasting their success and good fortune.

From his conning tower lookout, Marinesko watched the bright orange explosions as three of his torpedoes struck the ship's hull a few feet beneath the surface. He didn't know at that point that the ship was the *Wilhelm Gustloff*, carrying thousands of German civilian refugees. It wouldn't have mattered if he had known. The ship belonged to his nation's most hated enemy, and he was duty bound to sink it.

What happened to the *Wilhelm Gustloff* that cold night in 1945 was horrific and historic. With a death toll of approximately 9,400 people, half of whom were children, the *Gustloff* sinking ranks as the worst sea disaster in history.[7]

And yet, for many years after the catastrophe, almost no one knew about it. Political leaders, and even survivors, simply didn't talk about it. The reasons for this long silence are many and complicated. But because of it, for nearly 60 years, the sinking of the *Wilhelm Gustloff* remained a mere footnote in a few history books. Only in recent decades have survivors felt ready to talk. The tragic and epic story of the *Wilhelm Gustloff* disaster has finally begun to emerge.

The Allies and the Axis

World War II in Europe was essentially a struggle between two groups of nations: the Allies and the Axis powers. The war began in 1939, when German dictator Adolf Hitler's seemingly unstoppable armies invaded Poland, Denmark, Norway, the Netherlands, Belgium, Luxembourg, and France in quick succession. In 1940, Germany, Japan, Italy, and several other nations joined forces to form the Axis powers. By 1941, following the Japanese attack on the naval base at Pearl Harbor, Hawaii, the United States joined with the United Kingdom, the Soviet Union, and other nations to form an opposing alliance—the Allies. The war between Allied and Axis forces lasted until 1945 and claimed an estimated 50 million lives worldwide.[8] It was by far the deadliest conflict in history.

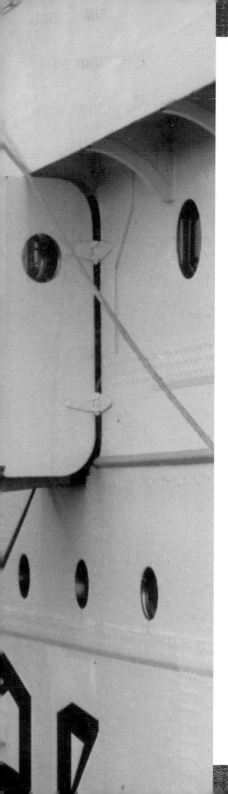

Chapter 2

STRENGTH THROUGH JOY

The story of the *Wilhelm Gustloff* began with Hitler's earliest days in power. One of his first actions after assuming control of Germany in 1933 was to disband all labor unions. He arrested labor leaders and grabbed the union dues collected from millions of German workers. He gave the money to the Deutsche Arbeitsfront (DAF), or German Labor Front. His government-run DAF, Hitler told workers, would look after them far better than their unions had ever done. The affected workers, who made up the vast majority of

the German population, were understandably angry. The DAF continued to deduct union dues from their pay but offered them virtually nothing in return.

Hitler had to do something before workers' grumbling and discontent turned into widespread protests or perhaps even open rebellion. To make his dream of world conquest come true, Hitler had to have an all-out effort from German workers. He came up with a plan to convince workers that his government was ready to reward them for their contributions and sacrifices in the workplace. It was called the Kraft durch Freude (KdF), or Strength through Joy, organization.

KdF, established in 1933 by DAF director Robert Ley, was designed to give ordinary people opportunities to relax and enjoy themselves away from their jobs. Previously, only the wealthy could afford to take part in leisure activities such as sports and travel. Now, the government said, everyone would be able to enjoy those things. It was billed as a way to close the gap between rich and poor. The concept of a community of people united and working together toward one goal was attractive in Germany. It was one of the key principles of Hitler's Nazi Party agenda.

KdF created all sorts of recreation opportunities. Loyal, productive workers could attend free government-sponsored theater productions, movies, exhibitions, concerts, and sporting events. They could also take part in folk and ballroom dancing lessons, tours and hikes, and a wide array of adult education classes.

Who Was Wilhelm Gustloff?

The founder of the Swiss Nazi Party, Wilhelm Gustloff, was assassinated on February 4, 1936, by David Frankfurter. The young student sought to call attention to Germany's inhumane treatment of Jews. Frankfurter was later sentenced to 18 years in a Swiss prison.[1] During Gustloff's elaborate, ritualistic funeral, Hitler called him a "sacred martyr" for the Nazi cause.[2] He also swore vengeance against "our Jewish foes," whom he blamed for most of Germany's and the world's problems.[3] Hitler's hatred and obsession resulted in the Holocaust.

Gustloff *by the* Numbers

The *Wilhelm Gustloff* was designed and built by a noted engineering firm, Blohm and Voss, in the firm's Hamburg, Germany, shipyards. The vessel was designed to carry approximately 1,500 passengers and a crew of 400. Driven by two enormous propellers, it weighed 25,484 short tons (23,119 metric tons) and was 684 feet (208 m) long and 77 feet (23 m) wide.[5]

By far the most attractive element of the program to most workers was its allowance for regular paid vacation time. It offered affordable travel packages, both inside Germany and to popular surrounding areas, such as the Mediterranean and Scandinavia. Many people who had never been able to travel before jumped at the chance.

Originally, KdF had nine ocean liners, older vessels that were about to be put out of commission. They were filled for nearly every voyage. Encouraged, Ley planned the construction of 20 additional vessels. The new ships would be advertisements for Hitler and his Nazi Party. They would be floating representations of the party's favorite slogan: "Ein Volk! Ein Reich! Ein Führer!," or "One People! One Empire! One Leader!"[4] In the summer of 1936, the keel was laid for the first ship, to be called the *Wilhelm Gustloff*. It was named for the founder and head of the Swiss Nazi Party, who had been assassinated in February that year.

Wilhelm Gustloff differed from other ocean liners. In keeping with its intended purpose, *Gustloff* was intended to have no first-, second-, or third-class accommodations. All of its

489 cabins were said to be essentially alike, conveniently placed on the outside of the ship and high above the waterline.[6] That way everyone, including the crew, enjoyed the same bright sea view and fresh ventilation from ample portholes. Passengers were free to roam the ship's eight levels, which provided almost 54,000 square feet (approximately 5,000 sq m) of deck space, as well as a wide promenade deck entirely enclosed in glass.[7] Also available to everyone was an indoor swimming pool, a movie theater, a gymnasium, two dining rooms, and several large common rooms for group gatherings. Everyone ate the same meals off the same fine china and sterling silver utensils engraved with the Nazi swastika.

Gustloff's builders made no claims about their vessel's resistance to attack. They did, however, widely publicize the ship's easily accessed, high-quality lifeboats. The ship would have 22 of them. The *Gustloff* also would have a double hull divided into 12 watertight bulkheads.[8] The double hull was particularly important, designers said. The *Titanic*, a much larger and supposedly unsinkable ship, had only a single hull, and it sank in 1912.

Painted a gleaming white with a red swastika on its single smokestack, the *Wilhelm Gustloff* was launched with an elaborate ceremony and rousing speeches on May 5, 1937. Thousands attended the gala event, including Hitler himself. The highlight of the ceremony was Ley's announcement of the ship's official name, presumably kept secret until that moment. Hedwig Gustloff formally christened the vessel named in honor of her late husband by breaking a

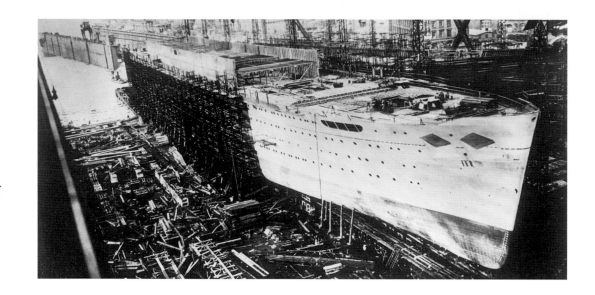

bottle of champagne across the bow. On March 29, 1938, the second new ship, the *Robert Ley*, was launched with similar fanfare. It was the *Wilhelm Gustloff*'s virtual twin.

Nothing quite like KdF had ever been done before, and most of the German people adored the program. By 1935, more than 3 million people had taken part in evening sports and gymnastics activities. An estimated 400,000 took KdF-sponsored voyages and trips. By 1937, that number grew to 1.7 million, and that same year, nearly 7 million people participated in shorter weekend tours and outdoor activities.[9] After the war, KdF was one of the few things many Germans remembered fondly about life in Nazi Germany.

The Turning Tides of War

KdF was essentially cancelled in 1939. That year, Hitler's armies invaded Poland, breaking an agreement he'd made earlier with the United Kingdom and setting off World War II in Europe. At that point, perhaps, the German people began to understand for the first time the high price they were going to have to pay for accepting Hitler and his Nazi regime. *Wilhelm Gustloff*'s service as a passenger liner ended with its final voyage to Norway in September 1939. Hitler announced he could no longer spare workers away from their critical jobs producing war materials and supplies.

Wilhelm Gustloff's ownership was officially transferred from the DAF to the Kriegsmarine, the German navy. A wide line of green was painted all around its hull, and the red swastika on its funnel was replaced with a red cross. *Gustloff* was officially redesignated as Hospital Ship D, staffed with doctors and nurses and sent to the eastern Baltic Sea to pick up and treat the growing number of

First Cruises

A few days after departing on its first practice cruise in the English Channel on April 2, 1938, the *Gustloff* answered a distress call from a British ship, the *Pegaway*. It was in danger of sinking in a terrible storm. A heroic effort by the *Gustloff*'s crew on April 4 rescued the *Pegaway*'s crew just before the ship sank.

From April 8 to 12, the *Gustloff* was sent to the United Kingdom on another mission. The *Gustloff* was anchored 50 miles (80 km) off England's coast. A great show was made over bringing selected Germans living in England aboard to vote on the issue of whether Austria should be forced to join with Germany. Everybody knew exactly how they were supposed to vote. In case they forgot, a heading on luncheon menus said, "Your Thanks for Voting Yes."[10]

soldiers wounded during Germany's invasion of Poland. Between April and June 1940, *Gustloff* went north to Norway to supply medical aid to soldiers injured during fighting there. On June 19, 1940, the ship left Norway for Germany filled with critically wounded men.

In November, the *Wilhelm Gustloff* was reclassified once again. This time, it was sent to the German naval stronghold at Gotenhafen, Poland. There the ship was painted drab gray and permanently moored to the pier. For the next four years, it served as a training vessel for German submarines, called U-boats. Trainees used it as a school and a barracks as they trained aboard submarines and other vessels in the Bay of Danzig and Baltic Sea. The commander in chief of the Kriegsmarine, Admiral Karl Dönitz, was convinced U-boats were Germany's most promising weapon.

As the years passed, new Allied tactics and technology neutralized Germany's powerful U-boat fleet. Hitler and his generals pinned their hopes on outlasting their enemies' will to fight and on the arrival of several new and technologically advanced weapons.

Showing Off

In May 1939, the *Wilhelm Gustloff* was showcased again as it and several other ships sailed to Spain to transport home an elite group of German troops, the Condor Legion. That unit helped Nationalist leader Francisco Franco win the Spanish Civil War (1936–1939). The troops were welcomed back to Germany with a celebration of speeches and cheering crowds.

They hoped new and more powerful planes, tanks, subs, rockets, and bombs would turn the balance of power back in Germany's favor.

Misery for Civilians

In the meantime, war was making life increasingly difficult for German civilians. An Allied naval blockade of the German coastline meant higher prices for goods. Shortages of nearly everything became the new normal. At the same time, workers' vacations vanished, along with bearable working hours and fair wages. In their place, the government instituted a seemingly never-ending series of higher production quotas and longer workdays. By 1940, Hitler's military and police forces controlled and oversaw nearly every aspect of peoples' lives. Constant surveillance and intimidation made any sort of resistance or relaxation dangerous. Slacking or failing to work with all one's might was treason, punishable by arrest, imprisonment, or death. Slowdowns or rest periods were out of the question. It was only the beginning of the deprivations and horrors to come.

Over the next few years, Germans learned what they'd actually bought with their DAF dues and their willingness to follow a dictator obsessed with war and world conquest. Between 1940 and 1942, Germany's powerful armies spread out, invading and conquering much of Western Europe. Poland, Denmark, Sweden, Finland, Belgium, Luxembourg, the Netherlands, and

Mini-Bio
Karl Dönitz
Admiral

Even before the war began, German admiral Karl Dönitz understood the potential of submarines as the basis of Germany's naval superiority. His U-boats became the terror of the seas. They might have even won the war if the Allies hadn't found a way to defeat them. Before Hitler killed himself at the end of the war, he named Dönitz the next leader of Germany. Days later, Dönitz surrendered to the Allies. Dönitz was arrested and tried, along with other Nazi leaders, for crimes against humanity. Dönitz refused to admit that he had any part in or knowledge of Germany's atrocities. He pointed to his role in saving refugees as reason enough to spare him. He was found guilty anyway and sent to prison, where he served a ten-year sentence. Before his death in 1980, Dönitz wrote his memoirs, *Ten Years and Twenty Days*. The title refers to the length of what he saw as his unjust punishment.

France all collapsed before Germany's powerful war machine. Italy and Japan embarked on their own bloody quests for power and territory. And other nations, including the United States and the United Kingdom, formed alliances in an effort to stop them. By 1943, nearly the entire world was engulfed in the war.

As is usually the case, the ones who suffered the most were the helpless millions of refugees who fled to escape carnage. During wartime, though, the suffering of noncombatants means very little to those in charge. In many cases during World War II, civilian refugees became the targets of some of the worst violence. Genocide and the extermination of civilian populations became a part of the war.

The End Draws Near

By January 1945, Hitler's delusions and poor tactical decisions had stretched his available manpower and resources too far. His once unbeatable military, called the Wehrmacht, was exhausted. They were running out of nearly everything—food, ammunition, equipment, and even soldiers fit enough to fight. Most Germans knew the regime was on its last legs as the Allies closed in, with US and British armies coming from the west and Soviets coming from the east. Still, Hitler and the Nazi leadership refused to give up. They ordered Germans to resist, to stand and fight to the death for the Fatherland.

<anchor ∴> *As soldiers, tanks, and bombers destroyed towns and villages, civilians either died or survived to live among the rubble.*

When the Soviet Red Army broke through German defenses in East Prussia on January 12, hundreds of thousands of civilians made a mad dash for freedom and life, unwilling to die for a lost cause. Yet Nazi security police and officials in the area still refused to let them go. When a few people tried to leave, police turned them back. They even shot some people who tried to sneak away. It was a terrible moment for Germans in East Prussia, many of whom had been sent there against their will. Hitler needed them there to work in factories and mines, they were told.

As the days passed and the Red Army drew closer, people began panicking. News arriving ahead of the Soviets was almost too horrific to believe. Soviet soldiers were torturing and killing German soldiers and civilians alike. Proof arrived in the form of photos and film taken in the town of Nemmersdorf after the Red Army steamrollered through it. The images were circulated all over East Prussia by the Nazi propaganda office. The disturbing images showed men and women nailed to the sides of houses and barns. They showed the brutalized bodies of children in the fields where they had been shot and clubbed to death or run over by Russian tanks. They showed families that had been incinerated in their own homes and people literally cut to pieces if they ran. "This, my countrymen, is what awaits you if you surrender," German authorities told them in radio and print messages.[11] The meaning behind the words was clear. German leaders expected their people to die fighting rather than surrender or flee.

⚓ *Germany sent young boys and old men to East Prussia in late 1944 to build up the region's defenses.*

ESCAPING THE FRONT

According to historian Richard Overy, "Hitler's obsessive self-belief consumed everything in its path, including the prospect of a more sensible strategy. German defeat was not just caused by Hitler; he ensured that defeat, when it came, would be total and devastating for the German population."[1] A concrete illustration of this is Hitler's refusal to allow Germans to retreat ahead of the advancing Soviet Army until the last possible moment. Indeed, for days and weeks, in spite of the mounting carnage and terror, Hitler refused to give orders to allow East Prussian civilians to evacuate. Many local leaders continued to hang their hopes on the appearance of miracle weapons still in development or in Hitler's ability to spring a brilliant, last-minute tactical surprise. Government propaganda had hinted that Hitler was purposely allowing the Soviets to advance deep into East Prussia. It implied he would soon spring shut the trap and annihilate vast numbers of Soviet invaders.

"Electro-boats"

At the end of 1944, the German navy launched a new type of submarine that drew in fresh air through a long pipe, or snorkel. Since the subs didn't have to surface as often, they weren't easy to detect by Allied radar or lookouts in ships or planes. Germany's best chance was these subs, known as "electro-boats." They were intended to be much faster and more powerful than anything the Allies had. As late as January 1945, Hitler and the German military still believed mass production of the new supersubs might save Germany from certain destruction.

Hitler eventually had no choice but to allow people to retreat ahead of the crushing onslaught. But he still urged them to resist at every opportunity. "Lash out in all directions with fists and claws to gain control of the storm sweeping over the eastern borders," he urged during one radio broadcast.[2] In another, he expressed his utter contempt for people who refused to fight to the death. "If the German people should collapse under the present burden, I would weep no tear after it. It would deserve its fate."[3]

In East Prussia, regional governor Erich Koch ordered women and children to dig anti-tank trenches in fields outside of towns and villages. He also sent the local Volkssturm, or German national militia, to defend against the Soviet advance. Civilians, many of them young boys and old men, were sent to front line positions with no training and minimal weapons. They stood no chance against veteran soldiers of the Red Army. Soviet soldiers killed Volkssturm recruits by the hundreds and mutilated their bodies to terrorize the population.

By mid-January, civilians and soldiers were in full retreat. German security police and members of the Hitler Youth organization watched streets and roads for anyone else traveling illegally. Based on instructions from the German capital, Berlin, even fleeing civilians were now considered military deserters. Many were shot, some on their very doorsteps when they set out without passes or permission. Many thousands huddled in their homes, wondering what to do.

In the town of Elbing, 40 miles (64 km) east of Danzig, ten-year-old Horst Woit and his mother Meta

Hitler Youth

The Hitler Youth was a paramilitary organization for boys and girls, created to instill Nazi principles in children and young adults. Activities combined fun and games with lessons about German superiority and the persecution of minorities, especially Jews. Younger members sometimes served as office pages, messengers, aides, and errand runners. Older youth were frequently used by the military in those same tasks. Hitler Youth were also trained to inform on people, including their own family members, who did not adhere to patriotic Nazi standards of behavior or speech. By 1939, 82 percent of Germans ages 10 to 18 belonged to Hitler Youth groups.[4]

Mini-Bio
Horst Woit
Child Refugee

Similar to thousands of other child refugees aboard the *Gustloff*, ten-year-old Horst Woit was less concerned with war and politics than he was about the little things he left behind. He missed marmalade and butter sandwiches and his small toys back home. While the Red Army set about destroying their city, Horst and his mother joined others racing across the Vistula Lagoon, a frozen body of water beside the Baltic Sea. Just before the Red Army cut off their last means of escape, the Woits made it to Pillau and caught a ferry to Danzig. Several days later, when Horst was pulled from the icy Baltic Sea, someone offered him a butter and marmalade sandwich. Yet, as he ate it, he felt that the peace and stability that small treat had always represented were gone. The things he'd experienced had changed him forever.

were among those anxiously waiting. Finally, on the morning of January 26, a boy in a Hitler Youth uniform pounded on their door. Soviet tanks had entered the town, he said. They had to leave at once.

Meta Woit had had a suitcase packed for weeks. They had to travel light, so she told Horst not to take anything. But when she wasn't looking, he slipped a jackknife into his pocket. At least he'd have something useful to remind him of home.

Wrapped in multiple layers of clothes against the bitter cold, Meta and Horst hurried away. They joined thousands of other panicked refugees clogging the fields and roads. Their trek was a nightmare. They ran in the freezing cold, dodging Allied attacks from the air and on the ground. Everywhere along the way they passed piles of possessions refugees dropped and the bodies of people young and old killed by the Red Army or who died from exposure or starvation. Days later, they reached Gotenhafen and joined a chaotic struggle in the streets to reach the docks before the last ships sailed.

Goth's Haven

The Polish port city of Gdynia became Gotenhafen after Hitler invaded in 1939. *Gotenhafen* means "Goth's haven" in German. Goths were modern Germans' early ancestors, whose warlike ways Hitler admired. His conquests were attempts to wipe out anyone who was not Aryan, his term for pure-blooded Western Europeans, descendants of Goths. He particularly targeted Eastern Europeans, especially Jews. Hitler killed vast numbers of Poles and Jews and relocated people he considered pure-blooded Germans east to occupy their cities and homes. Changing the names of Gdynia and dozens of other places in conquered countries to new Germanic ones was just one small part of Hitler's master plan.

Operation Hannibal

The massive wave of humanity converging on the town of Gotenhafen the last week of January 1945 was made up of people from all parts of the eastern Baltic region. Many had come a long way already, not just from cities and towns in East Prussia, but also from West Prussia, Pomerania, Silesia, Croatia, Latvia, and Lithuania. Some were even prisoners of war, recently released or escaped from German camps.

There were German military men and women along with their families, too. They had been released like everyone else to find a way to get out. Others were German soldiers wounded in recent fighting. Many of them couldn't walk on their own, relying instead on others, professionals and volunteers alike, to assist them. All of them were part of the most massive sea evacuation effort ever attempted. Called Operation Hannibal, the rescue was orchestrated by the German navy. It was the only branch of Hitler's once-invincible military with enough men and resources left to even attempt such an immense effort.

Operation Hannibal was carried out under the direction of Admiral Dönitz. His desire to keep the U-boat station at Gotenhafen open as long as possible was one reason it took so long for the order to evacuate to be given. He had supported Hitler's resistance to any mention of a massive Baltic area rescue.

But by the third week of January, Dönitz realized he could wait no longer. He had to get his submariners out of East Prussia before the Soviets captured them. On January 21, 1945, Dönitz sent a single-word message, *Hannibal*. The code word triggered the launching of the evacuation, which began on January 23.

The navy began rounding up every vessel available and sent them to Gotenhafen. By the final week of January, the harbor and pier were jammed with a variety of watercraft, including fishing trawlers, freighters, cutters, and dinghies. If it could float and had an engine, it was ordered into service. Especially important to the operation were the large submarine training ships that had been moored at Gotenhafen for much of the war—*Wilhelm Gustloff, Hansa, Hamburg, Deutschland,* and *Cap Arcona*. Each ship would be pressed to carry thousands of people more than its peacetime capacity.

Admiral Dönitz placed Commander Wolfgang Leonhardt in charge of the operation at Gotenhafen. From his office overlooking the harbor, Leonhardt coordinated everything. Even as *Gustloff*'s crew worked frantically to prepare the ship for service, he sent dozens of other vessels on their way, packed with military and civilian refugees.

It was the latter group that made Leonhardt's job so difficult. He knew almost exactly how many military men and women needed evacuating. But he could find no accurate way to estimate or control the surging civilian crowds that constantly besieged the remaining ships. Gotenhafen was jammed with thousands of desperate people with no adequate food or shelter, all frantically pushing into the harbor area. Looting and violence were rampant all over the city.

The situation on the docks quickly spun out of control. There was virtually a riot every time a ship lowered its ramps. Hungry, panicked people trampled one another rushing the gangplanks. Some even tried to climb the ships' sides. Guards and crews could do little to stop them. Ships filled to bursting before they could get out of the harbor. One ship, the *Cap Arcona*, sailed west with 14,000 passengers, nearly ten times its designed capacity. The *Deutschland*, a former cruise ship, took 12,000. Yet, somehow, dangerously overloaded ships made the trip safely west to Kiel and other German cities. By the end of January, Operation Hannibal had already successfully transported an estimated one million people to safety. But at least one million more still waited.[9]

Chapter 4

⚓ *The ship's expansive recreation areas would soon fill with bustling masses of refugees.*

BOARDING

With each passing day, the frenzied mob on the pier watched the *Wilhelm Gustloff* with ever-growing desire and apprehension as its crew rushed to get the ship ready. The noise of battle on the outskirts of the city and the terror of bombs raining down constantly increased people's fear and desperation. No one knew how long the patched-together German defenses could hold. By January 30, with most of the larger ships already gone, it seemed to most of the remaining 60,000 or so refugees that the *Gustloff*, the biggest of them all, might be their last hope of survival.[1]

Wilhelm Gustloff's chief officers were Commander Wilhelm Zahn and Friedrich Petersen. Petersen was essentially a civilian.

A merchant ship captain, Petersen had been in charge of the *Gustloff* almost from the beginning. Zahn was a hard-nosed military commander in charge of the submarine divisions aboard the ship. Zahn took orders directly from Admiral Dönitz and transferred them to Petersen and his staff. To Commander Zahn, the military aspect of the evacuation was most important. As Hitler did, he refused to accept the idea that the war was over. Getting his submariners—with their collective knowledge, training, and skills—to safety was a first step toward getting them back into the fight. He also took a personal interest in transporting as many critically wounded soldiers and seamen as possible back to Germany. They were his comrades in arms. They'd given their all for the Fatherland, and they deserved a better fate than to fall into the hands of the Soviets. Next came Nazi officials and the families of military officers of all branches. Any remaining space would be filled with as many civilian refugees as could be crammed in—women and children first, then adult men.

A Hopeless Situation

"At all fronts the enemy is advancing while we are unable to offer serious resistance to him . . . [and] in the East entire armies are dissolving or are hopelessly hemmed in. . . . Meanwhile, the Cossacks and the hordes of foreign workers are turned loose on our women and children. Germany is bombed into rubble and ashes and no one will build it up again."[2]

—*From propaganda leaflets dropped from Allied planes, urging German troops and civilians to surrender*

Flotation Gear

Life jackets were vital safety features in short supply as the *Gustloff* prepared to sail. During early boarding, passengers were each issued a life jacket. However, as thousands more people than expected poured aboard, the supply of flotation devices apparently ran out. Men were instructed to give theirs to women and children. By departure time, less than one-half of the people on the ship had one.[3] Many who did either didn't know how to properly wear and adjust life jackets or chose not to. As events later proved, improperly worn flotation devices may have been more deadly than not wearing any at all.

Gustloff was not in particularly good shape, so getting it ready to sail again took some work. Its engines had not run in more than four years. Mechanics labored for days without rest to prime the ship's fuel and boiler systems, lubricate rusty cogs and bearings, and ensure that parts that had not moved in years would operate smoothly again. The ship's upper decks and hull had sustained some damage during repeated Allied bombings as well. Most worrisome, two days before the ship was supposed to sail, it had only 12 of its 20 original lifeboats still hanging in their proper places. Crews of other evacuation boats that had already sailed had taken the others. The boats they took were the large and sturdy ones capable of carrying more than 120 passengers each. The builders had hyped them as one of the *Gustloff*'s strongest safety features.

The *Gustloff*'s crew found new boats to replace them. Soon, they had gathered 18 small rowboats used by U-boat trainees in and around the harbor. They didn't fit the *Gustloff*'s specially made davits. The new boats were simply tied to the decks.

Aside from those things, the *Gustloff*'s passenger cabins, kitchens, dining areas, and common rooms were clean and in good condition. Crews and trainees had lived and worked in these spaces continually over the years. The whole procedure was made somewhat easier, too, since most of the ship's approximately 2,000 naval personnel had been reassigned. Some went to other Operation Hannibal ships, while others were sent to the outskirts of Gotenhafen to help defend the city and harbor while the evacuation was underway.

In the final days before departure, the *Gustloff*'s remaining crew worked frantically to find as much room as possible for passengers. Tables and chairs were removed from dining areas, meeting rooms, and the movie theater. Decks, closets, stairwells, hallways, and every other nook and niche were cleared of debris and nonessential furniture and gear. People escaping deadly peril would not require or expect the same level of comfort KdF tourists once enjoyed. With that fact in mind, the crew drained the indoor swimming pool as well. That valuable space alone would accommodate hundreds. The glass-enclosed promenade deck encircling the ship was set up as a hospital.

⚓ *Emptying the ship's common areas of furniture created more room for the thousands of passengers clamoring to get aboard.*

Squeezing In

The first passengers began coming aboard the *Gustloff* while final preparations were still underway. Some military personnel were allowed to board almost a week before civilian refugees. One group that arrived early were 373 female members of the German navy. They were girls and women who served in various noncombat roles supporting military operations. Some sent to the *Gustloff* were trained as medical assistants. A number of them were conscripts, civilians drafted into service in a wide variety of noncombat jobs. They were thankful for the opportunity the big ship provided to escape the approaching Red Army. The Soviets' treatment of German women and girls had been particularly vicious.

Among the girls was 18-year-old Eva Dorn. Although she was happy to be leaving turmoil and danger behind, she didn't like the looks of the *Wilhelm Gustloff.* She thought it was too big and too easily seen by enemy planes or warships. "I didn't feel safe, and I had a bad feeling," she told an interviewer years later.[4]

Another teen, Rose Rezas, was another draftee into noncombat military service. Rose was 19 and had worked as a military telephone operator and helped build anti-tank obstacles in a northern village before she was told to leave. It was the chaos and devastation in Gotenhafen that had disturbed her the most when she arrived five days before the *Gustloff* sailed. Bodies lay untouched in the streets and among the rubble of bombed out buildings. She and her father were fortunate to get safely aboard before another crushing wave of refugees arrived. Rose was assigned to the huge ballroom with other women and girls, while her father was sent elsewhere. Getting comfortable lying on the rock-hard dance floor was not easy. But anything was preferable to having to sleep outdoors in the cold and dangerous city like so many other refugees.

The day before the *Gustloff* sailed, officials began issuing fewer boarding passes. People on the docks knew what that meant. Word spread that the ship would sail at any time. It set off a frantic push by remaining refugees to get aboard by any means possible. People aboard began to pass babies and young children to childless people on the docks. Hundreds used that ploy and got aboard in the final hours. Some deserting German soldiers dressed like women and tried to carry borrowed children aboard. Others carried rolled up blankets to mimic the shapes of sleeping babies. Guards and military police stopped most of them. Those they caught were usually shot or hanged in public view as grim warnings to others.

The *Gustloff*'s crew quickly and efficiently packed passengers into the spaces they'd created for them all over the ship. As the hour of its sailing approached, the *Gustloff* seemed almost to bulge and sag from the excess weight, one crew member recalled. Heinz Schön was a 19-year-old purser's assistant. He recalled that

Going It Alone

German naval officials made every effort to provide evacuation ships from Gotenhafen and other ports with protection. Several battleships, gunboats, torpedo boats, and minesweepers were tasked with escorting refugee ships when they sailed. In the *Gustloff*'s case, officers of the submarine division, waiting impatiently aboard, overruled objections from those in charge of assigning evacuation escorts. They refused to wait a day or two for strong defensive vessels to return from previous trips west, instead ordering *Gustloff* to sail virtually unescorted.

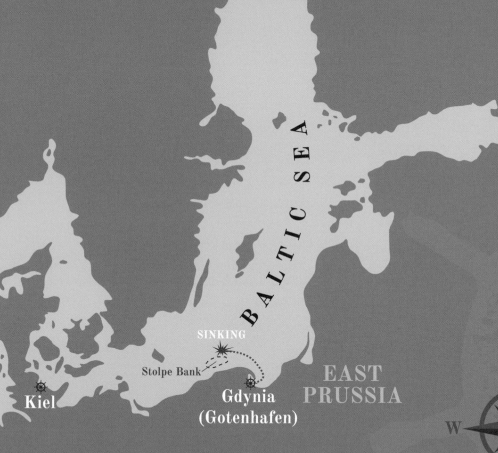

THE BALTIC SEA AND EAST PRUSSIA

BALTIC SEA

SOVIET
UNION

Moscow ⚓

SINKING

Stolpe Bank

EAST
PRUSSIA

Gdynia
(Gotenhafen) ⚓

Kiel ⚓

Berlin ⚓

GERMANY

the uproar on the pier grew louder and more pitiful when the plank was pulled in and the crew prepared to cast off. Desperate parents began to hand and even throw their young children to crew members or anyone else on board. Some children fell into the icy water and drowned before they could be rescued. Risking their babies' lives this way seemed preferable to exposing them to the horrors of the looming Soviet menace.

Even then, the rush was not over. As the *Gustloff* drifted away from the pier and angled out into the harbor, a small flotilla of boats followed. Refugees screamed for people to let down ropes and nets and allow them to climb the steep sides. Although it was officially frowned upon, Schön later noted, perhaps as many as 2,000 additional refugees succeeded in getting on board in this way at the last moment.[5]

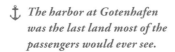
⚓ *The harbor at Gotenhafen was the last land most of the passengers would ever see.*

A STORMY DEPARTURE

Carrying approximately 10,000 people, the *Gustloff* officially set sail at 1:00 p.m. on January 30, bombarded by a sudden hailstorm.[1] With it went the *Hansa*. That seemed fitting, since the ship was also a submarine training vessel and had shared the same pier as *Gustloff* for the past several years. It carried approximately 3,000 refugees, as well as the submarine division's equipment and gear.[2]

Despite the bitterly cold and stormy weather, the *Gustloff*'s passengers and crew were tremendously relieved to finally be

"This Fateful Battle"

"The horrid fate now taking shape in the east . . . that exterminates hundreds of thousands in villages and market places . . . will be warded off in the end and mastered by us. . . . In this fateful battle there is therefore for us but one command: He who fights honorably can thus save his own life and the lives of his loved ones. But he who, because of cowardice or lack of character, turns his back on the nation shall inexorably die an ignominious death."[3]

—*From a live radio address by Adolf Hitler broadcast over the* Gustloff's *public address system to passengers the night of January 30, 1945*

underway. In keeping with the spirit of its original design and construction, nearly everyone on board shared equally cramped and uncomfortable quarters. But given the alternative—facing the brutal Red Army—few people complained. Almost as soon as the *Gustloff* cleared the harbor entrance, most people, exhausted and stressed from their torturous ordeals, settled down to rest.

As for Horst Woit and his mother, they had been exceedingly fortunate. They shared a cabin with only two others. As soon as possible, the ten-year-old set out to explore the ship. For him, the whole evacuation experience so far was an exciting adventure. He scampered about, sticking his nose into every crevice and corner. Exhausted and frostbitten people were everywhere, many of them using the life jackets they'd been issued as pillows or mattresses.

The hundreds of young women from the German navy were lodged in the drained swimming pool area near the very bottom of the ship. They had each been issued a real mattress and pillow. That did not make their accommodations any more comfortable, however. The crowded, noisy quarters and lack of ventilation made the tiled space stifling and claustrophobic. Eva Dorn quickly decided that living in a stuffy, echoing cave for several days with more than 300 excited and animated young girls was not for her. She looked around and found a fresher, quieter place several decks above in the infirmary. Her medical training and eagerness to work made her a welcome addition to the staff. This decision almost certainly saved her life.

Stepping out on deck during a rare break, Dorn felt the intense cold as the ship departed the sheltered harbor. She also noticed the thick layer of ice forming on the metal deck plates and on the lifeboats. The davits and ropes, in fact, were frozen solid. Hail, blowing snow, and frigid temperatures had frozen together a number of inflatable rafts, too. There were 380 of them aboard, strewn about here and there. The replacement flotation vessels had been added at the last minute to take the place of the ship's missing lifeboats. Emergency measures were far from the minds of most of the passengers and crew.

After the ship reached the deeper waters of Danzig Bay, strong winds and high waves made the going considerably rougher. Soon large numbers of passengers became seasick. Unable to go outside onto the treacherously icy decks, people were forced to deal with their nausea inside.

Reserved for VIPs

A number of Nazi Party officials were aboard when the *Gustloff* set sail. The Kreisleiter of Gotenhafen, a low-ranking party official, along with his wife and five children, took one of the nicer cabins on the top deck. A luxury Führer Suite had been designed for Hitler's personal use but had never been occupied previously. Thirteen members of the family of the Burgomeister of Gotenhafen filled it that night for the first time. That official, who was something like a mayor, did not go with his family. He stayed behind to assist those defending Gotenhafen from the Red Army, and he died days later in the fighting.

Soon the ship reeked, and those who were not sick initially quickly became so. The crew worked diligently to help. On their recommendation, the sickest people moved inward toward the center of the ship. There, passengers didn't feel the rock and roll quite so violently. All over the ship, in an effort to get more comfortable, passengers unbuckled or removed their life jackets. A general calm and quiet settled over the ship.

Discord on the Bridge

That was not true of the bridge, however, where an argument was taking place. Two German naval officers, Heinz Weller and Karl-Heinz Köhler, had come aboard just before the *Gustloff* left. They assumed they would be in charge of sailing the ship. But Zahn and Petersen believed they themselves were in charge. The crux of the conflict was confusion over exactly what type of ship the *Gustloff* was. Was it a naval troop transport, a hospital ship, or a civilian refugee liner? Did the antiaircraft guns that had been mounted on its decks make it a warship? Technically, the *Gustloff* was all of those things. That complicated the matter of which captain was chief and which were subordinate. Petersen was essentially a commercial and peacetime officer. He was the *Gustloff*'s captain during the old KdF days. The others, particularly Zahn, were military men. None of them liked being told what to do by a merchant captain.

One of the points of debate was the speed at which the ship should be sailing. Zahn believed it was safer to sail at the fastest speed the ship had been designed for. That was 16 knots, or 18 miles per hour (29 kmh). Petersen knew the ship's engines were not in good condition due to long inactivity. He argued that 12 knots, or 14 miles per hour (22 kmh), was all the engines could handle.[4]

They also argued over which route to take. A course close to the shallow coast could expose them to mines. Deeper water farther from land risked attack from submarines or airplanes. They disagreed, too, about whether the ship should take a straight or zigzag course. The latter made it harder for submarines to hit them with torpedoes. But Petersen was not in favor of a zigzagging course. The Baltic Sea was congested with evacuation ships and their escorts. He was worried about a midsea collision in the darkness. They finally agreed on a deep-water course that had previously been cleared of mines. Petersen refused to zigzag. Zahn insisted on turning

⚓ *Petersen had served aboard the* Wilhelm Gustloff *for several years by 1945.*

on the *Gustloff*'s red and green navigation lights so that approaching ships would be able to see them and steer clear.

In addition to the *Hansa*, the *Gustloff* was accompanied by the *Löwe*, an old torpedo boat, and *TF-19*, a small craft that had been used to retrieve spent practice torpedoes in Gotenhafen Harbor. The crew of neither vessel had any escort training or experience. As the small convoy approached the Hela peninsula, a few miles from their departure point, *Hansa* developed engine trouble and *TF-19* sprang a leak. Both vessels had to turn back. That left *Gustloff* and *Löwe* alone and exposed as they forged on toward the open Baltic Sea.

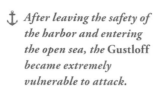

⚓ *After leaving the safety of the harbor and entering the open sea, the* Gustloff *became extremely vulnerable to attack.*

Chapter **6**

DEATH IN THE BALTIC

Nearly nine hours after its departure, just before nine o'clock, *Gustloff* was near the coast of Germany, approaching the Stolpe Bank gravel beds. Captain Weller prepared to take the helm as officer of the watch. The ship was moving nicely and the bickering on the bridge had ceased, at least for the time being. In fact, Captains Petersen and Zahn had retired to an officer's cabin and were having a bite to eat and a drink together.

Weller heard a loud explosion shortly after arriving on the bridge at 9:10 p.m. It lifted him off his feet and banged his head

into a metal doorframe. He thought at first the ship had hit a mine. Seconds later, two more explosions rocked the ship. He knew then it was a torpedo attack. Automatic alarm bells and sirens screamed and the *Gustloff* leaned sharply to starboard, the right side of the ship. Weller called the engine room to stop the ship, but it was no use. The third torpedo had exploded near the engine room, shutting down the machinery and killing most of the men working down there.

Asleep in his snug cabin, wearing an oversized life vest, Horst Woit didn't hear the first explosion. But he did hear the second one. He woke in time to feel the ship shake violently. He sat up and saw the look of terror on his mother's face. They were outside in the hallway, on the stairs to the upper deck, when the third torpedo struck. The concussion burst fire extinguishers hanging on the wall, spraying them and the steps with slimy chemical gel. They slipped on the mess and fell. As they struggled to right themselves, the stairwell filled with a mob of terrified, screaming people, pushing and clawing to get up the stairs and onto the deck and to the lifeboats.

Zahn and Petersen felt the ship heave to port, too. They rushed to the bridge, where Weller and other officers were meeting. Someone made an announcement on the PA system for passengers to go to the upper deck and not to panic. That instruction did little good. By the time the third torpedo struck, the ship was already pitching sharply to one side.

The officers did a quick damage check. The various captains gave orders to begin the closing of watertight bulkheads in the lower decks. The *Gustloff*'s hull was a shell divided into 12 separate compartments. Each could be closed off from the others by waterproof doors. It was important to quickly seal off any compartment where damage had occurred and water was pouring in. That would theoretically keep water from flooding the entire interior and sinking the ship.

Closing watertight doors was serious business. Once they were closed, people on the wrong side had no further hope of escape. In the case of the *Wilhelm Gustloff*, badly overcrowded as it was, that meant thousands of people would drown with the closing of every watertight door. But it could not be helped. Crew members were sent to the dark lower decks to assess damage and close doors as needed.

Damage below decks was extensive. The 660 pounds (300 kg) of explosives in each torpedo had ripped massive holes in the *Gustloff*'s hull.[1] The first torpedo had struck the ship near the

⚓ *The second torpedo struck near the swimming pool area.*

bow, just below the crew's quarters, where a large number of the *Gustloff*'s off-duty crew had been sleeping. The explosion killed hundreds. Many more were sealed alive in rapidly flooding forward compartments as watertight doors slammed shut. Nearly all of the more than 300 women in the drained swimming pool area were killed instantly by the blast of the second torpedo.[2] The explosion opened another gaping hole in the *Gustloff*'s hull.

The third torpedo struck amidships, near the center, close to the engine room. Many more of the ship's crew on duty there died instantly or drowned soon after as water gushed in through the ship's third massive gash. *Gustloff*'s engines were immediately swamped and the boat's main power supply failed. People on all levels were plunged into blackness. A crew member rushed to shut the watertight door for the compartment with the new hole, sealing the fate of anyone who might have survived the initial explosion. Nearly all of the lower decks quickly became tombs.

On the forward command deck, the ship's main radio transmitter had stopped working. The operator switched on an emergency set but it didn't work, either. Finally, he found an old army transmitter someone had stowed there. He switched it on and began tapping out telegraphic signals requesting assistance and giving the ship's position. It didn't accomplish much, since the backup radio's range was only approximately 1.2 miles (2 km).[3] The *Löwe* was the only vessel close enough to receive the message.

Fifteen or twenty minutes after the torpedoes hit, *Gustloff* was already leaning toward the port side at a 30-degree angle. The radical tilt, thick smoke, rising water, and interior darkness made escape from lower decks almost impossible. Emergency ladders were available, but almost no one except crew members knew where they were.

Hundreds who did find their way to upper decks still encountered problems. With skilled deck crews trapped far below, almost none of the lifeboats were launched correctly. Many could not be lowered because the davits and rigging were frozen solid. No amount of pounding and chipping could free them. Simply trying to walk on the sloping, ice-covered decks could be fatal. Many people slid into the icy water. Others suffocated in avalanches of bodies that tumbled and piled up against rails or items on the deck.

Horst Woit and his mother were fortunate enough to get into a lifeboat. But as it was being lowered, it suddenly stopped and hung, swinging wildly in the wind. The heavily loaded boat slammed into the ship's tilting side, nearly throwing everyone into the sea. Horst heard a man desperately shouting that the rigging ropes were snagged. He was pleading for something he could use to cut them. That's when Horst

Another Way Out

Survivors reported grim stories that people trapped aboard the *Gustloff* chose to commit suicide rather than face the torment of a slow and icy death. As the ship went down, survivors on deck and in lifeboats heard the unmistakable sounds of gunfire. One witness reported actually seeing a German naval officer shoot his wife and children before killing himself. Another man heard a woman begging her husband, "Put a quick end to us all!"[4] A second later, he heard the snap of pistol shots. Some people decided to end it another way. They stripped off their clothes before diving into the near-freezing water. They may have thought the cold shock would knock them out, allowing them a painless death.

Officers First?

Many survivors later reported that among the first to board the few available lifeboats were many of the ship's crew, including Zahn and Petersen. Members of the military, too, filled the first lifeboats, while thousands of civilians clamored for help on the deck. The behavior was likely based on the same mind-set that had determined the boarding priority of government officials, military officers, and war wounded first, then refugees. The German military was desperate for leadership in the final days of the war. Military people were seen as crucial to the continued war effort. Civilians were not.

remembered the jackknife. He'd nearly forgotten about it in the excitement. He fished it out of his pocket and passed it to the man, who slashed the ropes. The boat plummeted, somehow landing upright on the water.

As the lower decks of the ship filled with water, the *Gustloff* leaned farther and farther to port. Stressed beyond their limits, the ship's rivets, bulkheads, and steel braces began to fail. Wider cracks opened all along the hull.

Escape

By that time, mass hysteria was sweeping through the ship. Survivors recalled the pitiful howls and screams from people trapped below, scrambling for lifeboats, or helplessly slipping to their deaths on the ice-coated decks. The noise grew shriller, louder, and more urgent with each passing minute. Making it into a boat did not necessarily guarantee survival. Some passengers were crushed when heavy boats fell on them. Untold hundreds struggled to untie and inflate portable rafts stacked randomly around the decks. Dozens more found them insufficiently inflated and sank when they did get into the water.

Eva Dorn was working with a doctor in the upper deck infirmary when the torpedoes hit. Stunned, she instinctively dashed for the stairs. On the way, she passed a pile of flotation vests, grabbed one, and put it on. Moments later, she joined a line of people waiting to board a lifeboat. As she helped lift a woman and two children into the boat, another one next to it tipped suddenly and toppled overboard, dumping its load of terrified people into the sea. Eva climbed into her boat, wearing only her uniform and the life vest. Numb with fear and cold, she clasped two small children to her as the boat was lowered. On the surging waves, there was no one to steer the boat. Eva grabbed the lever that operated the boat's rudder. Somehow, the boat turned and drifted away from the *Gustloff*'s dangerously rolling hull.

Where Were the Life-savers?

Post-disaster inquiries cited the failure of crew members responsible for emergency tasks and duties as one major cause for the high death toll. The *Gustloff's* crew of skilled sailors was badly depleted from the start. To make matters worse, nearly all of those trained in firefighting, escape procedures, and launching lifeboats were sleeping in the crew's quarters in the bow of the ship, where the first torpedo struck. The crew members who might have saved thousands of lives had been killed in the initial explosion.

At approximately the same time, 16-year-old Eva Luck and her six-year-old sister Dorrit were trapped in the ship's music room. They dodged a runaway grand piano that careened across the sharply tilting floor. It crushed several people before it smashed to pieces against a wall. By the time the girls got free and onto the deck, the ship was lying almost on its side. Eva could see the ship's funnel angled down almost parallel with the sea. Icy waves cascaded over the deck, drenching her and Dorrit. Then a huge wave rolled over them, picking them up like toys. "I reached out to try and grab my sister," she said later. "I felt nothing but the water as it swept me out and over the side."[5]

Eva Luck, Eva Dorn, and Horst and Meta Woit were four of the small number of passengers who somehow managed to escape the *Gustloff*. They watched breathlessly as the ship's stern lifted and the ship slipped bow first into the depths. At the last moment before it disappeared, the ship's boilers exploded. Incredibly, the ship's lights, which had been out for nearly an hour, suddenly blazed brightly. The vessel's alarm sirens shrieked.

A Survivor's Memory

"I could clearly see the people on board the *Gustloff* clinging to the rails. Even as she went under they were still hanging on and screaming. All around us were people swimming, or just floating in the sea. I can still see their hands grasping at the sides of our boat. It was too full to take any more."[6]

—*Paula Knust, 23-year-old* Gustloff *survivor*

Other survivors, too, recalled the strange and eerie howl that filled the air as the ship disappeared. It was the combined noise of the ship's sirens and the dying groans of the many thousands who went to the bottom with it. "I have that always in my ears," Eva Dorn told an interviewer years later.[7] Approximately 62 minutes after the first torpedo struck the *Gustloff*, the enormous ship slipped beneath the waves. Three of its lifeboats were still hanging unused in their davits.[8]

Chapter 7

THE STRUGGLE FOR SURVIVAL

At the time the *Gustloff* sank, the air temperature was 4 degrees Fahrenheit (–16°C). For those in and out of the water, hypothermia became a deadly enemy. In such bitter conditions, it was only a matter of minutes before people in the water, along with wet people in lifeboats exposed to the wind, would die. Yet some kept themselves from slipping into unconsciousness. Furious rowing, swimming, struggling, and the sheer will to survive kept some alive long enough to be rescued. In a number of cases, there was simply no explanation why some survived and others perished.

Survivors later recalled that, once the ship was gone, a strange quiet settled over the area. From the lifeboats, people gazed at a surreal scene. A bright moon at times lit the water with a silvery glow. Other times, it ducked behind thick clouds and the sea was plunged into darkness. But even in the dark, those on the boats could hear the desperate cries of people in the water all around. Curtains of snow came and went, and chunks of white ice floated in the water.

Many of the lifeboats were seriously overcrowded. People who had been perfectly gentle and respectable under normal circumstances found themselves turned to savages, punching, slapping, kicking, and beating others with oars to keep them away from their overfilled lifeboats. In one boat, armed military men opened fire on swimmers who came too close.

Nineteen-year-old Rose Rezas faced such an ordeal. She and her sister Ursula escaped the *Gustloff* almost at the last minute by breaking a porthole and squeezing through. In the freezing water, without life jackets, the

Danger on the S-13

As soon as Commander Marinesko saw the deadly impacts of his torpedoes on the *Gustloff*, he immediately gave the order to dive. He didn't know the *Gustloff*'s escort had so little firepower. And even if he had known, he still had a serious problem. He'd fired four torpedoes, and only three of them had left the sub. The fourth remained jammed inside its firing tube. Luckily for *S-13*, *Löwe* didn't start firing depth charges until the sub was well out of the area. A minor noise or jostle, even the boom of a practice depth charge, might have exploded the torpedo and blown *S-13* to pieces.

girls were separated. Her hands and arms bleeding, Rose swam toward the nearest lifeboat. The passengers slapped at her and frantically tried to push her away. She fought back and climbed aboard anyway. There was no place to sit, so she lay in the bottom of the boat in sloshing, icy water. Her hair froze, and her pain grew so sharp she prayed she would lose consciousness.

Rescued!

The *Gustloff*'s only escort, the much smaller *Löwe*, was pushing forward in the heavy waves far ahead. Its crew did not recognize the larger ship's distress right away. The torpedo boat sailed on for several minutes before its lookouts noticed the *Gustloff* was no longer behind them. That's when they saw the red signal flares and came racing back. Their radio operator began sending out distress calls immediately.

Oddly, the first ship to hear of the disaster was incapable of responding. It was the *Hansa*, still disabled with engine trouble back at Gotenhafen pier. *Löwe*'s operator had neglected to switch his radio's frequency from that of the U-boat division headquarters. That mistake lengthened the time it took for help to arrive on the scene.

The heavy cruiser *Admiral Hipper* received radio word of the *Gustloff*'s distress and, shortly after, saw its flares in the distance. Along with the torpedo boat *T-36*, *Hipper* had left Gotenhafen four hours after the *Gustloff*. They purposely followed the *Gustloff*'s course in

order to overtake it with the intention of escorting it to port in Kiel. *Hipper* and *T-36* arrived on the scene just in time to watch as *Gustloff* disappeared beneath the surface. Naturally, survivors struggling in the water and those in lifeboats saw the *Hipper* as a lifesaver. It wasn't. The ship's officers had decided that stopping with enemy subs in the area was too dangerous. The cruiser's sides were too high and steep for most people to climb aboard, anyway. As it departed, its deep wake and churning propellers capsized lifeboats and killed people floundering in the water.

T-36 stayed on the scene, and along with the *Löwe*, the crew rescued as many survivors as they could safely

The Last Rescue

At dawn on January 31, Werner Fisch was aboard dispatch boat *VP-1703*, inspecting lifeboats for survivors. Fisch did not believe anyone could still be alive, but it was his job to find out, so he jumped into one more boat to check. He was examining frozen victims when he saw a small movement. Beneath one of the bodies was a tiny baby, blue with cold, but still alive. Wrapped in a blanket aboard *VP-1703*, the baby was revived and doctors later declared the little boy perfectly fit. Fisch later adopted the baby, the youngest survivor of the *Wilhelm Gustloff.*

Who Was Responsible?

At a board of inquiry several days after the disaster, Zahn denied any responsibility for the *Gustloff* sinking. He blamed Petersen's refusal to accept his suggestions about course and speed as a primary cause. He also blamed the large number of Croatians on board, replacements for the usual crew members who had been reassigned elsewhere. Zahn said the non-German-speakers either didn't understand orders given to them, or they simply failed to carry them out. In the end, the board made no official ruling about cause or responsibility.

bring aboard. Afterward, both ships circled the area, firing their rounds of mostly practice depth charges. They didn't know if any enemy subs were still in the area. They just hoped the explosions would frighten away any subs that might still be lurking about. The only noticeable effect of the noisy blasts was to frighten and, in a few cases, kill some people still floundering in the water. The ships left after midnight, carrying approximately 800 survivors.[1]

Soon after, other ships began to arrive, but hauling everyone to safety took time. Many people died in their lifeboats, soaked to the skin or thinly dressed, waiting for rescue. As the night wore on, more and more rescuers found lifeboats filled with still and frozen bodies. In the sea, later rescuers also discovered large islands formed by the bodies of frozen people in life jackets.

A disturbingly large number of them were children, floating upside down, stiff legs sticking straight up. An unknown number of children had been packed aboard the *Gustloff* without parents or responsible adults. They were given flotation gear, but in many cases, the jackets were too large or incorrectly fastened. Once again, the presence of trained emergency personnel on deck during the evacuation might have saved the lives of many thousands.

By morning light, rescue boats had given up finding any more survivors. One writer described the terrible scene aboard one vessel, collecting the dead. "Children, mothers, fathers were stacked like cordwood on the boat's decks. There weren't enough rough wool blankets to drape all the corpses."[2]

Not all stories ended so tragically. After they were taken aboard the *Löwe*, Horst and Meta Woit were separated, each taken to different areas to be treated and fed. Once she began to recover, Meta went looking for Horst. When she couldn't find him, she

The Steuben *and the* Goya

Just 11 days after sinking *Gustloff*, Commander Alexander Marinesko and his *S-13* crew attacked another converted passenger liner, the *General Steuben*. That German refugee ship sank in the Baltic Sea approximately 45 miles (73 km) from the site of the *Gustloff* disaster. Of the estimated 5,000 people on board, only 659 survived.[3] On April 16, 1945, three weeks before the war ended, a different Soviet sub torpedoed the *Goya*, killing 7,000 passengers, mostly refugees and wounded soldiers. *Goya* went down in only four minutes, so quickly that just 183 people survived.

began to panic. She asked crew members, who thoughtlessly took her to a pile of bodies on the foredeck. The sight of so many dead children made her frantic. None of them was her child, but she couldn't rid her mind of the terrible picture. Finally, near dawn, Meta found her son sleeping among other male survivors.

Diagram of the
Wilhelm Gustloff

Bridge

Crew's
Quarters

First
Torpedo

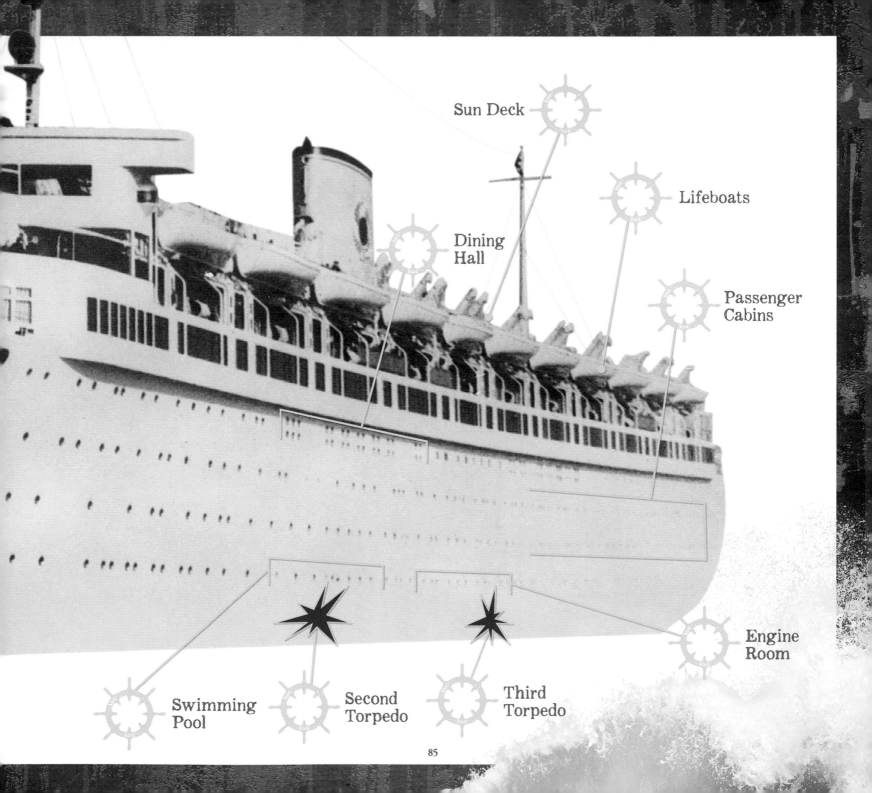

Sun Deck

Lifeboats

Dining
Hall

Passenger
Cabins

Engine
Room

Swimming
Pool

Second
Torpedo

Third
Torpedo

Survivors of the disaster, such as Guenther von Maydell, have kept the ship's story alive.

A FORGOTTEN STORY

For weeks after the disaster, bodies from the *Gustloff* kept washing up on beaches along the Baltic coast. Terrible though it was, the sinking of the *Wilhelm Gustloff* was just one more tragic event at a time when horror and death had almost become commonplace. Nothing like World War II had ever happened before. In the early months of 1945, people in Europe were in a state of shock, staggered and stunned by the devastation still going on around them. People in the United States and other countries far from the

The Official Report

"In connection with the sinking of the passenger steamer *Wilhelm Gustloff* by submarine torpedoes. . . . Painful as any loss may be, it is very fortunate that more have not occurred. However, [I] must point out that Russian submarines are able to operate undisturbed in the Baltic Sea only because there are no German aircraft there to combat them. Because of the shortage of escort forces the Navy must restrict itself to direct protection of convoys. The only practical defense against submarines is the radar-equipped aircraft, the same weapon which enabled the enemy to paralyze our own submarine warfare."[1]

—*From the official report of Karl Dönitz at the Conference on Naval Affairs, Berlin, January 31, 1945*

carnage found it hard to imagine the sheer scale of human suffering that had occurred. The full extent of the genocide, the mass killings of millions of Jews and others in Hitler's extermination camps, was just beginning to become known. The world was numb and war-weary, sick of death and senseless killing. In North America at the time it happened, news of the sinking of a German ship filled with enemy soldiers and war refugees was simply not seen as particularly noteworthy. *Gustloff*'s sinking rated only a passing mention on the back pages of a few papers.

In the *Gustloff*'s case, the rapidly collapsing German empire suppressed nearly all mention of the incident. News of the catastrophe first reached victims' families and friends mostly by whispered rumors. An official blackout of bad news was in effect in 1944 and 1945, a last-ditch effort by Hitler to hide the truth of his utter failure as a leader. The *Wilhelm Gustloff* was a symbol of German might and success, and its destruction was emblematic of the sinking of the Nazi dream. There was also a growing feeling among the German people that perhaps they deserved such catastrophes. Maybe it was their just reward for supporting Hitler and his deluded plans. Keeping quiet became a national obsession. In late March, following artillery strikes on the city, the Red Army seized Gotenhafen (Gdynia). Hitler killed himself on April 30. On May 8, Germany surrendered to the Allies. World War II in Europe was over.

The Soviets kept the disaster, similar sinkings, and their role in these events a secret as well. With their victory over Germany, the so-called Cold War began. The Soviet Union entered a rivalry with its wartime ally, the United States. The events of the past five years quickly faded in importance. In the political struggle that followed, the Soviets were the inheritors of tremendous new power and territory. The evolution of the Soviet Union into a world power had begun. The United States and the rest of the Western world watched the rise of Soviet communism with a sense of fear and uncertainty. Looking at the *Gustloff* catastrophe in this historical context, historian Cathryn Prince evaluated its significance this way: "As the great ideological wall [divided] Europe and the cold war froze into place, the fate of a boatload of German civilians and military refugees had little importance."[2]

Eventually, the division between the Soviet Union and the Western powers became a physical barrier. The Berlin Wall, erected by the Soviets in the 1960s to split Germany's capital

War Crime or Military Target?

The sinking of the *Wilhelm Gustloff* has gone down in history as the largest maritime disaster ever. However, some say that the ship was a fair target. They point out that the ship was carrying a large number of German naval personnel and was armed with antiaircraft guns. Even though there were wounded aboard, it was not marked as a hospital ship. Thus, as writer Gunter Grass wrote in 2003, "They said the tragedy of the *Gustloff* was a war crime. It wasn't. It was terrible, but it was a result of war."[3]

into the Soviet-controlled East and the Western-controlled West, trapped and isolated East Germans psychologically and physically. Soviet control and censorship in East Germany were brutal and oppressive. East Germans, especially *Gustloff* victims, simply could not talk about the terrible atrocities the Red Army had committed against them. On the western side of the wall, survivors kept quiet for other reasons. Mostly, it was because nobody seemed interested in hearing any more stories of war tragedies.

The result of all this suppression was that a kind of dark curtain was draped over the story of the *Wilhelm Gustloff* disaster. Its banishment from history was so complete that more than 50 years later the story still rated barely more than a footnote in histories of World War II.

Loss of Life aboard the Wilhelm Gustloff

One of the unanswered questions about the *Wilhelm Gustloff* disaster is exactly how many lives were lost. In her 2013 book, *Death in the Baltic*, historian Cathryn Prince cites *Gustloff* assistant purser and survivor Heinz Schön. She states that "more than 9,000 people perished."[4] A television documentary aired by the Discovery Channel in 2003 used computer simulations to recreate the disaster. That program estimated the totals at 1,230 survivors, 9,343 dead, and 10,573 people aboard.[5] The data in this graphic is based on those estimates.

● 9,343 dead　　● 1,230 survivors

The Scars of War

After their rescues, *Gustloff* survivors were quickly scattered back into the general German population during the final days of the war. Most were terribly traumatized by what they'd experienced and seen. Talking about it all just brought back the painful memories. It was easier in the early aftermath to just keep silent.

There was another reason for their hesitance to talk. After the war, the German people struggled mightily to come to grips with what had happened. The scale of retribution, the payback dealt out by the Western Allies against Germany in the final days of the war for all its arrogance and cruelty, was enormous. One estimate lists 4 million German military and more than 600,000 civilian deaths during the conflict. The war created approximately 12 million civilian refugees in Eastern Europe.[6]

Return to the Gustloff

Gustloff survivor Heinz Schön dedicated his life to documenting the experiences of others who escaped from the ship. Before he died in April 2013, Schön asked professional diver Matthias Schneider to take him back there again. In November of that year, Schneider placed an urn containing Schön's ashes on *Gustloff*'s wreck. The container, which was made of salt, dissolved after a few days, distributing Schön's ashes across the ship and the surrounding sea floor. Schneider also attached a stainless steel plaque engraved with the words, "*Wilhelm Gustloff,* sunk on 30 January 1945. Rest in peace, Heinz Schön, 3 June 1926 to 7 April 2013."[7]

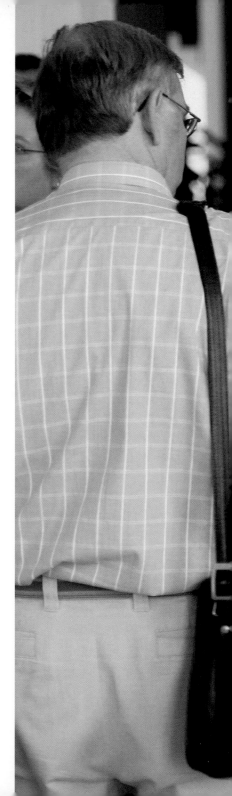

⚓ *Some recovered parts of the* Gustloff, *such as its bell, have been put on display in museums.*

The opinion by most non-Germans in the postwar world was that the German people were responsible for this suffering. The majority of Germans agreed. According to historian Ian Kershaw, many millions of Germans knew the details of Germany's role in the Holocaust, the death camps, and the atrocities committed in the Soviet Union and other European countries. Speaking of his own people, one postwar German writer asked, "What was it actually that drove us to follow [Hitler] into the abyss like the children in the story of the Pied Piper? The puzzle is not Adolf Hitler. We are the puzzle."[8] Nobel Prize–winning author Gunter Grass put it this way: "Because the crimes we Germans are responsible for were so dominant, we didn't have the energy left to tell of our own sufferings."[9]

The *Wilhelm Gustloff* survivors, nearly all of whom were Germans, were caught in this web of guilt, too. Their guilty silence had another layer. They were experiencing something psychologists call "survivor guilt."[10] A form of post-traumatic stress disorder, the term refers to intense feelings frequently seen in people who have survived disasters or violent crimes. Such people may believe that somehow they don't

Wilhelm Gustloff in Pop Culture

Several propaganda films were made at the time of *Wilhelm Gustloff*'s launching in order to promote the ship as a gleaming symbol of Nazi socialism and German pride. Long after the sinking and the end of the war, the ship appeared in dramatized productions. A popular movie treatment of the disaster was *Nacht fiel uber Gotenhafen* (*Night Fell Over Gotenhafen*), produced in German in 1960. Much more recently, *Die Gustloff* (*The Gustloff*) was a 2008 two-part movie made in Germany. In addition to Grass's 2002 novel *Crabwalk*, another significant book about the *Gustloff* is Ruta Sepetys's 2016 young adult novel, *Salt to the Sea*. That book tells the tragic story through the eyes and in the words of four fictional characters.

⚓ Gustloff *survivor Heinz Schön,* left, *posts with a cast member on the set of the 2008 German movie about the sinking.*

deserve to be alive, that they have no right to speak of their own suffering, or that they must demonstrate their regret and worthiness to live. That is exactly what many Germans felt in the decades after World War II.

Over time, however, the need to face the past became an overwhelming necessity. In 2002, Grass published a novel, *Crabwalk*. At the core of Grass's fictional story was the very real one of the *Wilhelm Gustloff*. After the novel appeared, an article titled "The German *Titanic*" appeared in the popular German magazine *Der Spiegel*. The article praised Grass and his novel for finally opening the door and giving Germans, particularly *Gustloff* survivors, the opportunity finally to talk about feelings and tell stories that had been taboo for decades. The 2015 book *Death in the Baltic*, written by Cathryn Prince, includes the stories of a number of *Gustloff* survivors. Many of them were speaking on the record about their extraordinary experiences for the first time. One of them was Horst Woit, who in his seventies finally got the opportunity to tell the world about his experiences on a bitterly cold January night in 1945.

Timeline

1933

⚓ In November, Robert Ley establishes the Strength through Joy (KdF) program.

1936

⚓ On February 4, David Frankfurter assassinates Wilhelm Gustloff, head of the Swiss Nazi Party.

1937

⚓ On May 5, the *Wilhelm Gustloff* is launched with much fanfare.

1938

⚓ On April 2, the *Wilhelm Gustloff* embarks on its first voyage.

⚓ On April 4, the *Wilhelm Gustloff* rescues the crew of the sinking British ship *Pegaway*.

⚓ From April 8 to 12, *Gustloff* is anchored off the coast of the United Kingdom to allow German citizens in England to vote on the issue of Austria's union with Germany.

1939

⚓ In May, the *Gustloff* and other ships bring home Germany's victorious Condor Legion from the Spanish Civil War.

⚓ In September, *Gustloff* becomes a German navy hospital ship and is sent to the Baltic Sea to take on wounded people from Germany's invasion of Poland.

1940

⚓ Between April and June, *Gustloff* assists wounded from Germany's invasion of Norway.

⚓ In November, *Wilhelm Gustloff* is reassigned as an accommodation ship and sent to Gotenhafen to house German naval trainees. It remains moored there for several years.

1945

⚓ On January 12, the Soviet Red Army breaks through German defenses and enters East Prussia.

⚓ On January 23, Operation Hannibal, Germany's evacuation of millions of refugees from the Eastern Baltic region, begins.

⚓ On January 30, *Gustloff* is sunk by torpedoes fired by the Soviet sub *S-13*.

⚓ On February 10, the *General Steuben* is sunk by *S-13* approximately 45 miles (73 km) from the site of the *Gustloff* sinking.

⚓ On April 16, the *Goya* is sunk by Soviet submarine torpedoes approximately 70 miles (113 km) from the *Gustloff* disaster site.

⚓ On April 30, Adolf Hitler takes his own life in a Berlin bunker. His will names Admiral Karl Dönitz new president of Germany.

⚓ On May 8, Germany agrees to a complete and unconditional surrender to Allied powers, ending the war in Europe.

1990

⚓ Alexander Marinesko is given the award of Hero of the Soviet Union, the nation's highest honor.

Essential Facts

What Happened

Wilhelm Gustloff, a German ocean liner that was converted during wartime for military purposes, was sunk by Soviet submarine *S-13.* An estimated 9,400 passengers died, making it the deadliest maritime disaster in history.

When It Happened

The *Gustloff* sank in the closing months of World War II in Europe, on the evening of January 30, 1945.

Where It Happened

The sinking occurred in the Baltic Sea, approximately 25 miles (40 km) north of the coast of Pomerania, at the Stolpe Bank.

Key Players

⚓ Commander Alexander Marinesko was the captain of the Soviet submarine *S-13.* He sank the *Gustloff* and the *Admiral Steuben* and posthumously earned the honor of Hero of the Soviet Union.

⚓ Admiral Karl Dönitz, commander in chief of the German navy, organized Operation Hannibal, the largest sea evacuation in history.

⚓ German dictator Adolf Hitler was the supreme leader of the German Nazi regime.

Legacy

For nearly 70 years, few people discussed the sinking of the *Wilhelm Gustloff*. Suffering from survivor's guilt after the war, the German people in general and the *Gustloff* survivors in particular felt compelled to keep silent. Finally, in 2002, publication of Gunter Grass's novel *Crabwalk* opened the door for discussion of those issues. The book dealt directly with the *Gustloff* disaster and German feelings of guilt. Since then, Germans have begun to speak more openly about their experiences during the war, and *Gustloff* survivors have come forward to share their stories.

Quote

"I could clearly see the people still on board the *Gustloff* clinging to the rails. Even as she went under they were still hanging on and screaming. All around us were people swimming, or just floating in the sea. I can still see their hands grasping at the sides of our boat. It was too full to take on any more."

—Paula Knust, 23-year-old Gustloff *survivor*

Glossary

atrocities
Acts of extreme cruelty or inhumanity.

conning tower
A raised platform from which an officer can give directions to a helmsman.

davit
The crane-like device and machinery used for raising and lowering lifeboats.

genocide
The deliberate mass murder of a group of people.

Holocaust
The systematic killing of millions of Jews by the Nazi regime during World War II.

hull
The frame or body of a ship, excluding masts, sails, and rigging.

hydrophone
A sensitive device used aboard ships and submarines for listening to underwater sounds.

hypothermia
The condition of having an unusually low body temperature.

martyr

Someone who is killed for a religious or political cause.

paramilitary

Organized similarly to a military force, but operating outside of a standard military command structure.

promenade

A space designed for walking and relaxation.

propaganda

Information that carries facts or details slanted to favor a single point of view or political bias.

starboard

The right side of a ship when looking forward.

surveillance

Close observation or watch kept over something or someone.

swastika

An equilateral cross with four legs each bent at 90 degrees; the symbol of the German Nazi Party.

Additional Resources

Selected Bibliography

Dobson, Christopher, John Miller, and Ronald Payne. *The Cruelest Night*. Boston, MA: Little Brown, 1979. Print.

Prince, Cathryn J. *Death in the Baltic: The World War II Sinking of the* Wilhelm Gustloff. New York: Palgrave Macmillan, 2013. Print.

Further Readings

Adams, Simon. *World War II*. London: DK, 2014. Print.

Mihulka, Krystyna. *Krysia: A Polish Girl's Stolen Childhood During World War II*. Chicago, IL: Chicago Review P, 2017. Print.

Sepetys, Ruta. *Salt to the Sea*. New York: Philomel, 2016. Print.

Online Resources

Booklinks
NONFICTION NETWORK
FREE! ONLINE NONFICTION RESOURCES

To learn more about the *Wilhelm Gustloff*, visit **abdobooklinks.com**. These links are routinely monitored and updated to provide the most current information available.

More Information

For more information on this subject, contact or visit the following organizations:

National Holocaust Museum

100 Raoul Wallenberg Place SW
Washington, DC 20024
202-488-0400
ushmm.org

The Holocaust Memorial Museum seeks to inspire people of all ages to confront hatred, prevent genocide, and promote human dignity.

National World War II Museum

945 Magazine Street
New Orleans, LA 70130
504-528-1944
nationalww2museum.org/about-the-museum/world-war-ii-links.html

Designated by Congress as the official World War II museum of the United States, this museum tells the story of why the war was fought, how it was won, and what it means today.

Source Notes

Chapter 1. Terror in East Prussia

1. Volker Wagener. "70 Years On, Little Known about the *Wilhelm Gustloff* Sinking." *Deutsche Welle*. Deutsche Welle, 30 Jan. 2015. Web. 14 Aug. 2017.

2. Christopher Dobson, John Miller, and Ronald Payne. *The Cruelest Night*. New York: Little Brown, 1979. Print. 23.

3. Cathryn J. Prince. *Death in the Baltic: The World War II Sinking of the* Wilhelm Gustloff. New York: Palgrave Macmillan, 2013. Print. 37–38, 43–44.

4. Victor J. Kamenir. "Naval Mines in the Baltic Sea." *Warfare History Network*. Warfare History Network, 26 July 2016. Web. 14 Aug. 2017.

5. Cathryn J. Prince. *Death in the Baltic: The World War II Sinking of the* Wilhelm Gustloff. New York: Palgrave Macmillan, 2013. Print. 101, 127.

6. Ibid. 96–97.

7. Ibid. 1.

8. Max Hastings. *Inferno: The World at War, 1939–1945*. New York: Knopf, 2011. Print. xv.

Chapter 2. Strength through Joy

1. Nicki Peter Petrikowski. "Wilhelm Gustloff." *Encyclopaedia Britannica*. Encyclopaedia Britannica, 24 May 2016. Web. 3 Apr. 2017.

2. Christopher Dobson, John Miller, and Ronald Payne. *The Cruelest Night*. New York: Little Brown, 1979. Print. 30.

3. Ibid.

4. Cathryn J. Prince. *Death in the Baltic: The World War II Sinking of the* Wilhelm Gustloff. New York: Palgrave Macmillan, 2013. Print. 55.

5. Edward Petruskevich. "The Man and the Ship." Wilhelm Gustloff *Museum*. *Wilhelm Gustloff* Museum, n.d. Web. 14 Aug. 2017.

6. Henrik Ljungström. "*Wilhelm Gustloff*, 1938–1945." *Great Ocean Liners*. Great Ocean Liners, n.d. Web. 14 Aug. 2017.

7. Cathryn J. Prince. *Death in the Baltic: The World War II Sinking of the* Wilhelm Gustloff. New York: Palgrave Macmillan, 2013. Print. 31.

8. Edward Petruskevich. "The Man and the Ship." Wilhelm Gustloff Muscum. *Wilhelm Gustloff Museum*, n.d. Web. 14 Aug. 2017.

9. Richard J. Evans. *The Third Reich in Power*. New York: Penguin, 2005. Print. 467.

10. Cathryn J. Prince. *Death in the Baltic: The World War II Sinking of the* Wilhelm Gustloff. New York: Palgrave Macmillan, 2013. Print. 57.

11. Ibid. 45.

Chapter 3. Escaping the Front

1. Richard Overy. "Foreword." *The Hitler Book: The Secret Dossier Prepared for Stalin from the Interrogations of Hitler's Personal Aides*. New York: Public Affairs, 2005. Print. xvi.

2. "Vain Attempts to Halt Soviet Advance, Germans Fortifying Berlin." *The Advocate*. National Library of Australia, 27 Jan. 1945. Web. 14 Aug. 2017.

3. Cathryn J. Prince. *Death in the Baltic: The World War II Sinking of the* Wilhelm Gustloff. New York: Palgrave Macmillan, 2013. Print 43.

4. Ibid. 31.

5. Alan W. Palmer. *The Baltic: A New History of the Region and its People*. Woodstock, NY: Overlook, 2006. Print. 372.

6. Charles W. Koburger. *Steel Ships, Iron Crosses, and Refugees*. New York: Praeger, 1989. Print. 92.

7. Alan W. Palmer. *The Baltic: A New History of the Region and its People*. Woodstock, NY: Overlook, 2006. Print. 372.

8. Cathryn J. Prince. *Death in the Baltic: The World War II Sinking of the* Wilhelm Gustloff. New York: Palgrave Macmillan, 2013. Print. 172.

9. Christopher Dobson, John Miller, and Ronald Payne. *The Cruelest Night*. New York: Little Brown, 1979. Print. 73–74.

Chapter 4. Boarding

1. Cathryn J. Prince. *Death in the Baltic: The World War II Sinking of the* Wilhelm Gustloff. New York: Palgrave Macmillan, 2013. Print. 121.

2. Ibid. 80.

3. Ibid. 117–118.

4. Ibid. 53.

5. Ibid. 121.

Source Notes Continued

Chapter 5. A Stormy Departure

1. Christopher Dobson, John Miller, and Ronald Payne. *The Cruelest Night.* New York: Little Brown, 1979. Print. 59–60.

2. Ibid. 52.

3. Cathryn J. Prince. *Death in the Baltic: The World War II Sinking of the* Wilhelm Gustloff. New York: Palgrave Macmillan, 2013. Print. 131.

4. Christopher Dobson, John Miller, and Ronald Payne. *The Cruelest Night.* New York: Little Brown, 1979. Print. 90.

Chapter 6. Death in the Baltic

1. Cathryn J. Prince. *Death in the Baltic: The World War II Sinking of the* Wilhelm Gustloff. New York: Palgrave Macmillan, 2013. Print. 131.

2. Ibid. 133.

3. Christopher Dobson, John Miller, and Ronald Payne. *The Cruelest Night.* New York: Little Brown, 1979. Print. 102–103.

4. Ibid. 111.

5. Ibid. 117.

6. Ibid. 62, 120.

7. Cathryn J. Prince. *Death in the Baltic: The World War II Sinking of the* Wilhelm Gustloff. New York: Palgrave Macmillan, 2013. Print. 143.

8. Irwin J. Kappes. "The Greatest Marine Disaster in History . . . and Why You Probably Never Heard of It." *Military History Online.* Military History Online, 2003. Web. 14 Aug. 2017.

Chapter 7. The Struggle for Survival

1. Christopher Dobson, John Miller, and Ronald Payne. *The Cruelest Night.* New York: Little Brown, 1979. Print. 130–131.

2. Cathryn J. Prince. *Death in the Baltic: The World War II Sinking of the* Wilhelm Gustloff. New York: Palgrave Macmillan, 2013. Print. 159.

3. Marcin Jamkowski. "Ghost Ship Found." *National Geographic.* National Geographic, Feb. 2005. Web. 14 Aug. 2017.

4. Ibid.

Chapter 8. A Forgotten Story

1. Christopher Dobson, John Miller, and Ronald Payne. *The Cruelest Night*. New York: Little Brown, 1979. Print. 136.

2. Cathryn J. Prince. *Death in the Baltic: The World War II Sinking of the* Wilhelm Gustloff. New York: Palgrave Macmillan, 2013. Print. 181.

3. Volker Wagener. "70 Years On, Little Known about the *Wilhelm Gustloff* Sinking." *Deutsche Welle*. Deutsche Welle, 30 Jan. 2015. Web. 14 Aug. 2017.

4. Cathryn J. Prince. *Death in the Baltic: The World War II Sinking of the* Wilhelm Gustloff. New York: Palgrave Macmillan, 2013. Print. 1.

5. Edward Petruskevich. "The Man and the Ship." Wilhelm Gustloff *Museum. Wilhelm Gustloff* Museum, n.d. Web. 14 Aug. 2017.

6. Gertrude Mackprang Baer. "Germans Wrestle with the Culture of Memory." *Toronto Star*. Toronto Star, 29 Apr. 2005. Web. 14 Aug. 2017.

7. Meiko Haselhorst. "Returning to the 'Gustloff' Was His Last Wish." *Die Welt*. Die Welt, 25 Nov. 2013. Web. 14 Aug. 2017.

8. Ian Kershaw. *The End: The Defiance and Destruction of Hitler's Germany, 1944–1945*. New York: Penguin, 2011. Print. 9.

9. Andrew Nagorski. "The German *Titanic*." *Newsweek*. Newsweek, 18 Mar. 2002. Web. 14 Aug. 2017.

10. Erik Kirschbau. "65 Years After WW2—Should Germans Still Feel Guilty?" *Reuters*. Reuters, 7 May 2010. Web. 14 Aug. 2017.

Index

Admiral Hipper, 77–79
Allied powers, 17, 28, 44, 89
Axis powers, 17

Baltic Sea, 6, 8–9, 11, 25, 26, 36, 38, 40, 52, 59, 61, 82, 87, 88
Barbarossa, Operation, 8
Berlin Wall, 89

Cap Arcona, 40, 41
Cold War, 89
Crabwalk, 96, 97

Deutsche Arbeitsfront (DAF), 19–20, 25, 27
Deutschland, 40, 41
Dönitz, Karl, 26, 28, 38, 40–41, 44, 88
Dorn, Eva, 49, 57, 71, 72–73

East Prussia, 6–8, 11, 30–31, 33–34, 38, 40, 52

flotation gear, 46, 56, 57, 58, 71, 76, 80
Frisch, Werner, 79

General Steuben, 82
German surrender, 28, 89
Gotenhafen (Gdynia), Poland, 5, 26, 37–41, 47, 49, 50, 52, 58, 61, 77
Goya, 82
Grass, Gunter, 90, 94, 96, 97
Gustloff, Die, 96
Gustloff, Wilhelm, 21, 23–24

Hamburg, Germany, 22
Hannibal, Operation, 38, 40–41, 47
Hansa, 40, 55, 61, 77
Hitler, Adolf, 6, 8, 17, 19–23, 25–29, 31, 33–35, 37, 38, 44, 56, 58, 88–89, 94
Hitler Youth, 35, 37
Holocaust, 21, 88, 94

Italy, 17, 29
Japan, 17, 29

Kiel, Germany, 41, 52, 79
Knust, Paula, 72
Koch, Erich, 34
Köhler, Karl-Heinz, 58
Kraft durch Freude (KdF), 20–22, 24–25, 47, 59
Kriegsmarine, 8, 11, 25, 34, 38, 40, 48, 57, 88

labor unions, 19
Leonhardt, Wolfgang, 41
Ley, Robert, 21, 22, 23, 24
lifeboats, 23, 46, 57, 64, 69, 70, 71, 73, 75–80, 85
Löwe, 61, 68, 76, 77, 79, 82
Luck, Eva, 72

Marinesko, Alexander, 9–14, 16, 76, 82

Nazi Party, 21, 22, 58
Norway, 17, 25, 26

Pegaway, 25
Petersen, Friedrich, 43–44,
    58–59, 63, 66, 70, 80
Poland, 5, 17, 25–27
propaganda, 31, 34, 44, 96

Red Army, 6, 8, 30–31, 35, 36,
    37, 49, 56, 58, 90
Rezas, Rose, 49, 76
Robert Ley, 24

S-13, 9, 11–14, 16, 76, 82
Salt to the Sea, 96
Schön, Heinz, 50, 53, 92, 93
Soviet Union, 8, 10, 17, 52,
    89, 94
Spanish Civil War, 26
Stalin, Joseph, 10
Stolpe Bank, 11, 52, 63
survivor guilt, 94

T-36, 77, 79
Titanic, 23, 97
torpedoes, 9, 11, 14, 16, 50, 59,
    61, 64, 66–68, 76, 77, 82, 88

U-boats, 26, 28, 38, 47, 77
United Kingdom, 17, 25, 29
United States, 17, 29, 87, 89

Volkssturm, 34–35

Wehrmacht, 8, 29
Weller, Heinz, 58, 63–64, 66
Wilhelm Gustloff
    boarding, 43–53
    construction, 22–24
    crew, 41, 43–47, 50–53,
        58–61, 66–68, 70–71
    evacuation, 64–73
    features, 22–23, 46–47,
        84–85
    lives lost, 92
    passengers, 48–53, 55–58, 64,
        69, 70–73
    sinking, 16, 66–73
    survivors, 75–83
    torpedo hits, 16, 63–64,
        66–68

Woit, Horst, 35, 36, 37, 56, 64,
    69, 72, 82–83, 97
Woit, Meta, 35, 37, 64, 69,
    72, 83

Zahn, Wilhelm, 43–44, 58–59,
    63, 66, 70, 80

About the Author

Michael Capek is a proud Kentuckian and former teacher. He's the author of many books for young readers, including *The D-Day Invasion of Normandy*. Michael's fascination with World War II stems from his childhood. His father served in Europe during the war, and the stories and the photos his father brought back sparked his imagination.